Down a River

Carole Telford and

Rod Theodorou

Heinemann Interactive Library
Des Plaines, Illinois

© 1998 Reed Educational and Professional Publishing

Published by Heinemann Interactive Library,
an imprint of Reed Educational & Professional Publishing Ltd,
1350 East Touhy Avenue, Suite 240 West, Des Plaines, IL 60018

Printed and bound in China

Illustrations by Stephen Lings and Jane Pickering at Linden Artists

Designed by Aricot Vert Design Ltd

01 00 99 98 97

10 9 8 7 6 5 4 3 2 1

Library of Congress Cataloging-in-Publication Data

Theodorou, Rod
    Down a river / Rod Theodorou and Carole Telford.
        p.   cm. -- (Amazing journeys)
    Includes bibliographical references (p.   -) and index.
    Summary: Takes the reader on a journey along the mighty Missouri
-Mississippi River, describing physical features, animal and plant
life, how people use the river, and the importance of conservation.
    ISBN 1-57572-153-8 (lib. bdg.)
    1. Stream animals--Missouri River--Juvenile literature.   2. Stream
animals--Mississippi River--Juvenile literature.   3. Natural
history--Missouri River--Juvenile literature.   4. Natural history-
-Mississippi River--Juvenile literature.   5 Missouri River-
-Juvenile literature.   6. Misissippi River--Juvenile literature.
[1. Missouri River.   2. Mississippi River.   3. Rivers.]
I. Telford. Carole, 1961-   .   II. Title.   III. Series: Theodorou,
Rod. Amazing journeys.
QL155.T46 1997
508.78--dc21

                                                          97-13745
                                                             CIP
                                                              AC

Some words in the text are bold, **like this**. You can find out what these words mean by looking in the Glossary on page 28.

Acknowledgments

The author and publishers are grateful to the following for permission to reproduce copyright photographs:

Bruce Coleman Limited pp. 13 (top), 23 (bottom; EPL (Rob Visser) p. 27; Buddy Mays pp. 10, 11 (bottom), 13 (bottom), 15 (top and bottom), 26; NHPA (Daniel Heinclin) p. 23 (bottom); Oxford Scientific Films (Nick Bergkessee) p. 17 (top), (Alan and Sandy Carey) p. 21 (middle), (Daniel J. Cox) p. 11 (top), (Jack Dermid) p. 19 (top), (Pat and Tom Leeson) p. 21 (top), (Zig Leszczynski) p. 21 (bottom), (Joe McDonald) p. 19 (bottom), (E. Robinson) p. 25 (top); Rainbow (Dan McCoy) pp. 16, 17 (bottom).

Cover photograph: Magnum Photos

Our thanks to Rob Alcraft for his comments in the preparation of this book.

Every effort has been made to contact copyright holders of any material reproduced in this book. Any omissions will be rectified in subsequent printings if notice is given to the publisher.

Contents

Introduction   6

Journey Map   8

Birth of a River   10

Into the Rapids   12

Along the Valley   14

Awesome Meanders   16

Marshlands   18

The Flood Plain   20

Into the Swamp   22

At the Delta   24

Conservation and the Future   26

Glossary   *28*

More Books to Read   *30*

Index   *32*

Introduction

You are about to go on an amazing journey. We are going to travel along the mighty Missouri and Mississippi Rivers, two of the largest rivers in North America. You will start at the source of the Missouri in the Rocky Mountains and travel hundreds of miles past grasslands, until you meet the Mississippi River. You will continue traveling south, through marsh and swamp, until you reach the sea.

On the way you will see an amazing variety of birdlife, and many other different kinds of plants and animals. You will also learn about the life of a major river, how rivers begin and end, and how important they are for the health of the world.

The writer Mark Twain called the Mississippi "the crookedest river in the world."

Rivers always start on high ground and flow downward, toward a lake or the sea. The Missouri-Mississippi follows the same pattern. Like many rivers, its life is often compared to the life of a person. It spends its childhood rushing down high ground at speed, tumbling over rocks and waterfalls. When it becomes a grownup, it winds its way gently through valleys. Then it reaches old age, where it slows down until it finally ends its life at the sea.

The Missouri – Mississippi network forms the fourth largest river in the world.

CANADA

Rocky Mountains

Missouri

Mississippi

KEY

MISSISSIPPI RIVER

MISSOURI RIVER

UNITED STATES OF AMERICA

Mississippi Delta

GULF OF MEXICO

Journey Map

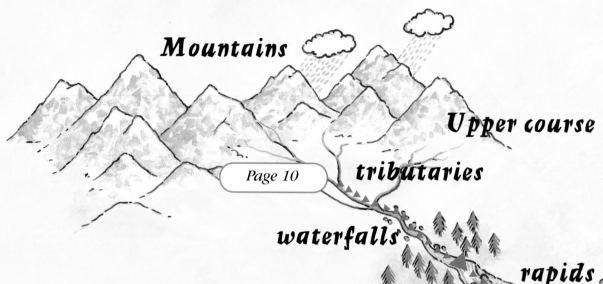

Mountains

Upper course

tributaries

Page 10

waterfalls

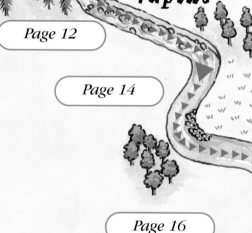

rapids

Page 12

Page 14

This map shows the three different sections of the river. Each section has a name. The upper course is the young river. The middle course is the grownup river, which winds its way along slowly like a giant snake. The lower course is the old river, where it divides into many smaller, slower rivers, and meets the sea.

Page 16

Page 18

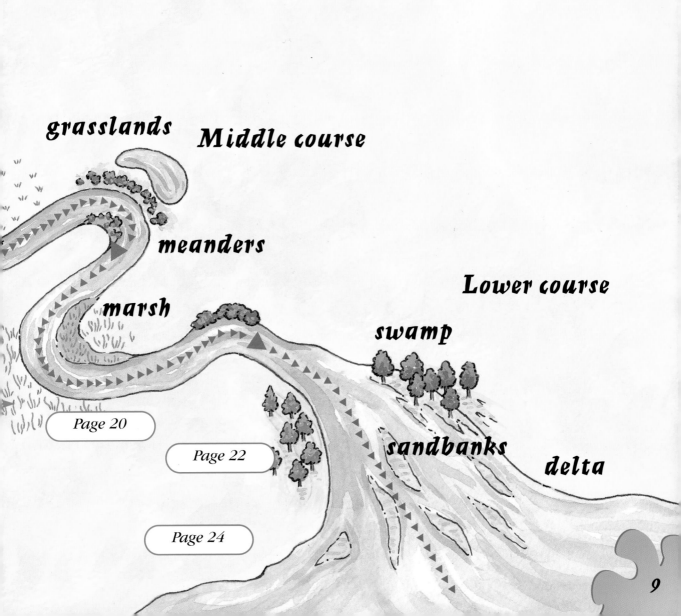

grasslands

Middle course

meanders

Lower course

marsh

swamp

sandbanks

delta

Page 20

Page 22

Page 24

Birth of a River

We are standing in the Rocky Mountains in the middle of a pine forest. The air is fresh but very cold. It has just stopped raining. We can hear the sound of rushing water nearby. We walk carefully over mossy rocks until we reach a fast-moving stream. The water is rushing down the high mountain, tumbling over rocks and **boulders**.

Below we can see where this stream meets other streams, called tributaries. Rain falls on the mountains, forming hundreds of tributaries. These join together to form a river. This is where the Missouri River starts. It is called its source.

This small tributary helps form the huge Missouri River.

Black bear →

This huge bear will eat almost anything. The black bear spends the winter in a deep sleep beneath a fallen tree or inside a cave at the source of the river.

Waterfalls

As the water flows over rocks, it cuts into them. Over thousands of years it cuts deeper and deeper into the hillside forming a V-shaped valley.

In very steep places, the fast water cuts into soft rock, but not into hard rock. This forms steps in the rocks. The river tumbles down these steps in waterfalls.

Into the Rapids

One of the most exciting ways to travel down this part of the river is in a **canoe**. We grip onto our paddles, pushing them into the water to keep our balance. We have to be very careful. The fast-flowing river is wild and powerful. It rushes through **canyons**, past white cliffs, swirling around hard rocks. Sometimes, it rushes over hundreds of **boulders** and small waterfalls. These are called rapids. The noise is deafening. We get soaked by the white foaming water.

You need a canoe or raft to travel through these rapids.

Rainbow trout

These fish are powerful and **streamlined** to survive in the fast-flowing water. Rainbow trout swim **upriver**, sometimes leaping up over the rapids and waterfalls.

Moose

In the summer this giant deer likes to enter shallow water to eat water plants and escape biting flies and **mosquitoes**. Moose are very good swimmers and can even dive under water to find tasty plants.

Golden eagle

Here among the canyons, we are lucky enough to see one of these **rare** and magnificent hunters on its huge nest. The nest may be as wide as a car! These huge birds hunt rabbits, prairie dogs, and even small deer.

Along the Valley

The river valley is much wider now. We travel past woods and **prairie** grasslands. With binoculars we can see a **prairie dog town**. Above the noise of the croaking frogs, we hear the howls of distant coyotes.

osprey

great horned owl

prairie falcon

prairie dogs

beaver

white-tailed deer

raccoon

wild turkey

bull snake

rock wrens

river otters

salamander

Beaver

The beaver is the biggest rodent in the United States. Beavers cut down small trees by **gnawing** them with their huge teeth. They use these logs and other sticks and mud to make huge **dams** across the river. By damming parts of the river, the beavers make ponds where they can live and build their homes, called lodges.

River otters

It is hard to catch sight of these shy animals. Sometimes, a family of river otters can be seen playing on the riverbank or sliding down mudbanks. Otters sometimes stand up on their two back legs to sniff the air for **predators**.

Prairie dogs

These animals live in hundreds of burrows called a town. Some of the prairie dogs act as lookouts, watching for enemies such as coyotes, eagles, or foxes. This dog is giving the "all-clear" signal, telling the others a predator has moved on.

Awesome Meanders

We have now entered the middle course of the river. The valley is flat so the river **current** has slowed down, but it is still powerful. Instead of cutting downward into the rock, it cuts sideways into the bank. This makes the river twist from side to side in huge bends called meanders. Soil from the banks enters the river making it muddy and full of rich **nutrients**. This helps more water plants to grow, which feed even more animal life. We see herons, some standing very still, some **wading** by the shallow banks.

Both the Missouri and the Mississippi have amazing meanders.

Ruby-throated hummingbird

This tiny bird flaps its wings so fast that they make a humming sound. Hummingbirds can **hover** and even fly backward. Their tiny nests are as small as eggcups.

Great blue heron

The largest bird in the United States, the great blue heron measures more than six feet across its wings! It wades through the water on its long legs looking for fish and frogs, which it spears with its long, strong beak.

Making meanders

As the river swings around a bend, it slices into the far side of the bank, cutting away the soil. While it is cutting one side of the bank, it dumps sand and stone by the other bank. This makes the bend bigger and bigger.

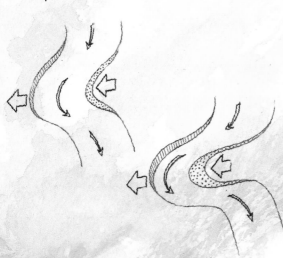

Marshlands

Further down the valley, the land is even flatter. In some parts, the river has no real banks at all. Water has spread into the surrounding area to form **wetlands**. When reeds and rushes grow over this wetland, it forms a **marsh**. Marshes are wonderful places for birds to hide and nest in.

yellow-headed blackbird

northern harrier

damselfly

bittern

reeds

muskrat

meadow vole

marsh wren

ruddy duck

garter snake

painted turtle

Mudpuppy

A mudpuppy is a large salamander that likes muddy or weedy waters. It eats crayfish, worms, snails, and other **aquatic** insects.

Bullfrog ⟶

The bullfrog is the largest frog in North America. It feeds on tadpoles, crayfish, salamanders, worms, and even mice or ducklings.

Muskrat

The muskrat looks like a huge rat with a large, flat tail, which it uses as a **rudder** to help it swim. If attacked, muskrats show off their big teeth or hide under water where they can hold their breath for up to twelve minutes.

The Flood Plain

The Missouri has at last met the mighty Mississippi. We take a ride on a **tug** heading south **downriver**. Much of this part of the river is channeled by stone walls, earth banks, and huge **dams**. We see other tugs pushing long columns of barges. We pass steelworks and other factories, as well as towns and cities.

The flat land around us is called the flood plain. If there is a year of heavy rains the river may burst its banks. Then all the towns, cities, and farmlands here may be in danger. The dams and wooded shorelines are not as wild as before, but they are still home to nesting birds. We catch sight of a pair of bald eagles circling overhead.

A dam on the Mississippi, built to control the height of the river to make it safer for boats and barges.

Bald eagle

Bald eagles spend the winter near dams. Their heads are not bald but are covered in white feathers. They can live for up to fifty years. They hunt small mammals, other birds, and fish.

Canada goose ⟶

Huge flocks of these large geese fly up the Missouri and Mississippi rivers to spend the summer in Canada. Sometimes, we see them with their young geese, called goslings.

Cottonmouth snake

The cottonmouth snake is **venomous** and may reach five feet in length. Its mouth is as white as cotton inside – but you only see this when it bites!

Into the Swamp

We are now in the hot, deep south of the country. Around us are huge **swamps**.

These **wetlands** are home to many unusual animals. We see turtles, terrapins, and snakes sunning themselves on logs. Then we see a log that moves! It's an alligator; the largest **reptile** in the United States!

Cypress trees

Spanish moss

hummingbird

blue heron

alligator

egret

terrapins

Alligator snapping turtle

The alligator snapping turtle stays under water at the bottom of the swamp with its mouth wide open. On its tongue it has a small piece of red flesh that looks like a worm. When fish swim up to eat the "worm", the turtle snaps them up with its powerful beak.

Alligator ⟶

Alligators are silent and very hard to spot in the still swamp waters. They grow up to 16 feet long and eat fish, turtles, and birds.

Crayfish

These small **crustaceans** fill the muddy water of the swamps and **bayous**. Crayfish are about as long as your hand. They are sometimes called mud bugs.

At the Delta

We are at the end of our journey. The old river has slowed so much it stops cutting into the banks and instead drops all the **silt** and mud it has carried along. These form **mudflats** and **sandbanks**. The river flows around these in hundreds of smaller channels, forming a huge delta. **Tidal** seawater washes up the delta. Worms and small **crustaceans** live in this salty mud, providing food for many shorebirds. They **wade** in the water and walk along the mudflats, digging for food with their pointed beaks.

The Mississippi "bird's foot" delta is one of the largest in the world.

Sandpiper

This busy little shorebird runs quickly, just ahead of the slow, lapping waves, probing for small animals. Sandpipers are often seen in large groups called flocks.

Great egret →

The great egret is a large, beautiful, white bird with a **crest** on its head. It stands very still in shallow water watching for small fish, then it darts its beak forward into the water like a spear to catch them.

Brown pelican

The brown pelican is a huge bird with a large bag or 'pouch' beneath its beak. It flies above the sea looking for fish, then it dives straight down. Just as it crashes into the water, it shoots its head and beak forward, catching the surprised fish in its pouch.

Conservation and the future

A river under threat. Along our journey we have seen hundreds of wonderful animals and plants. We have also seen how people use the river. We have seen huge factories that use up huge amounts of water. We have seen the **dams** and banks built to control the river and stop flooding. By stopping the **annual** floods many of the **wetlands** along the river have been drained and destroyed. The water in the river has also been **polluted** by factories and with **chemicals** used by farmers. This pollution kills many kinds of plants and animals.

Mississippi meanders have been straightened to make journeys quicker for tugs and barges.

Why are Rivers and Wetlands Important?

Only now are people realizing how careful we must be not to damage wetlands and rivers. Without **marshes** and **swamps**, many plants and animals may disappear for ever. Without meanders and **sandbanks** to slow the water, floods can be bigger and even more dangerous. One of the worst floods ever was in 1993. Whole cities were flooded and people and animals drowned.

The rivers we have traveled on flow through the heart of the United States. Like other great rivers, they act like the **blood vessels** in our bodies. They carry the water that all living things need to live. If we damage and pollute them, we damage ourselves.

The Mississippi flood of 1993 caused $10 billion in damage!

27

Glossary

annual	This means something happens once a year.
aquatic	This means to live in water.
bayou	This is a marshy area near a river.
blood vessels	These are tubes carrying blood through the body.
boulder	These are huge rocks.
canoe	This is a narrow boat.
canyons	These are deep channels cut into rock.
chemicals	These are liquids and sprays that have strong effects.
crest	This is a tuft of feathers sticking up on the head.
crustaceans	These are animals that have hard shells. Crabs are crustaceans.
current	This is the flow of a river.
dam	This is a wall that blocks the flow of a river.
downriver	This means in the direction that the river is flowing.
gnaw	This means to grind away with the teeth.
hover	This means to stay still in the air by flapping the wings very fast.
marsh	This is land that is always wet.
mosquitoes	These are small flying insects. Female mosquitoes bite and suck blood from animals and people.
mudflats	This is muddy land that is sometimes covered with water.
nutrients	These are parts of food that make living things healthy.

polluted	This means something is dirty or poisoned, usually by chemicals.
prairie	This is flat, grass-covered land.
prairie dog town	This is a network of homes, called burrows, where prairie dogs live.
predator	This is an animal that hunts and eats other animals.
rare	This means very few or hard to find.
reptile	This is a cold-blooded animal covered in scales.
rudder	This is a movable piece of wood or metal that steers a boat.
sandbanks	These are walls of sand.
silt	This is tiny pieces of rock and mud that settle at the bottom of a river.
streamlined	This means to be shaped to move through air or water easily.
swamp	This is land that is covered by shallow water.
tidal	This is the rise and fall of the sea.
tug	This is a boat that pulls or pushes bigger boats or barges.
upriver	This means toward the beginning of a river, or against the river's current.
venomous	This means something is poisonous.
wade	This means to walk through water.
wetlands	These are marshy areas of land.

More Books to Read

Ayer, Eleanor. *Our Great Rivers & Waterways.* Millbrook Pr. 1994.

Bailey, Donna. *Rivers.* Austin, Tex: Raintree Steck-Vaughn, 1990.

Bains, Rae. *Wonders of Rivers.* Mahwah, N.J.: Troll Communications, 1982.

Bender, Lionel. *River.* New York: Watts, 1988.

Cherry, Lynne. *A River Ran Wild:* An Environmental History. Orlando, Fla: Harcourt, 1992.

Crump, Donald J. *Let's Explore a River.* Washington, D.C.: National Geographic, 1988.

Cumming, David. *Rivers & Lakes.* New York: Thomson Learning, 1995.

Dabcovich, Lydia. *Follow the River.* New York: Dutton, 1980.

Emil, Jane. *All about Rivers.* Mahwah, N.J.: Troll Communications, 1984.

Hester, Nigel. *The Living River.* New York: Watts, 1991.

Nacona, George. *Riverkeeper.* New York: Macmillan, 1990.

Santrey, Laurence. *Rivers.* Mahwah, N.J.: Troll Communications, 1985.

Steele, Philip. *River through the Ages.* Mahwah, N.J.: Troll Communications, 1993.

The Earthworks Group. *50 Simple Things Kids Can do to Save the Earth.* New York: Jay Street/Little Brown, 1992.

Other Resources
Audio Recordings
Chapin, Tom. *Mother Earth.* A & M Records.

Raffi. *Evergreen, Everblue.* Troubadour Records.
Rogers, Sally. *Piggyback Planet: Songs for a Whole Earth.* Round River Records.

Video Recordings

Understanding Ecology Series: What is a Food Chain? Coronet © 1992.VHS, 11 minutes. (Also available on videodisk.)

Understanding Ecology Series: What is a Habitat? Coronet © 1991.VHS, 13 minutes. (Also available on videodisk.)

Understanding Ecology Series: What is an Ecosystem? Coronet © 1992.VHS, 11 minutes. (Also available on videodisk.)

Organizations

The Cousteau Society
70 Greenbrier Circle, Suite 402
Chesapeake,VA 23320
Tel (757) 523-9335

Greenpeace
1436 U Street NW
Washington, D.C.20009
Tel. (202) 462-1177

National Wildlife Federation
8925 Leesburg Pike
Vienna,VA 22184
Tel (703) 790-4100

Nature Conservancy
International Headquarters
1815 North Lynn Street
Arlington,Virginia 22209
Tel (703) 841-5300

River Watch Network
153 State Street
Montpelier,VT 05602
Tel (802) 223-3840

Sierra Club
85 Second Street, Second Floor
San Francisco, CA 94105-3441
Tel 415-977-5500

Index

alligator 22, 23

alligator snapping turtle 23

bald eagle 21, 20

beaver 15

black bear 11

brown pelican 25

bullfrog 19

Canada goose 21

canyon 12, 13

cottonmouth snake 21

coyotes 14, 15

crayfish 23, 19

dams 15, 20

flood plain 20

floods 27

golden eagle 13

great blue heron 17

great egret 25

meanders 17, 16

moose 13

mosquitoes 13

mudpuppy 19

prairie dogs 13, 14, 15

rainbow trout 13,

rapids 12, 14

river otter 15

Rocky Mountains 10

ruby-throated hummingbird 17

sandpiper 25

swamp 6, 22

tributaries 10

turtles 18, 22

valleys 7, 11, 14, 16

waterfalls, 7, 11

wetlands 18, 27